Nocturnes
A Passage of Dreams

Published by Shiel Street Press, Melbourne, 2021.

Copyright 2021 Brendan Gleeson

Cover image *Die Insel des Friedens,* Heinrich Vogeler, 1918–19

Cover design, layout and typesetting by Sharon France (Looking Glass Press)

Typeset in Stone Sans and Hammersmith One

All images sourced from Wikimedia commons

All rights reserved.

ISBN: 978-0-6453515-0-7 (paperback)
ISBN: 978-0-6453515-1-4 (e-book)

Dedication

These dream plays are for
My mothers
Through them
I was borne into the world

Die Rote Marie, Heinrich Vogeler, 1919

Acknowledgements

I thank my once wife
For bearing the children
And me
Along the way
Far enough

I thank Rheiner and Vogeler
And all like them
Especially Brian my father
For the inspiration of courage

Notes on Method

Always be a poet, even in prose
Charles Baudelaire

*The reason we go to poetry is not for wisdom,
but for the dismantling of wisdom*
Jacques Lacan

Contents

Nocturnes: A Passage of Dreams	1
The Central Players	19
Opening Scene, **the Mans Speak**	25
Dream Plays	27

    Arrow
    She Moved On
    The Wronged House
    The Black Sun
    Transgressions
    Global Sequence
    Tempus Fugitives
    A Drop Off
    One Act One Play
    The Beanstalk
    Nightwatchmen
    Flight of Fancy
    Unreeled
    Walking the Line
    Doing Time
    The Womans
    The Fool
    She Rules
    Second Dream Sequence
    Performances
    Dream with a Chaser

Intercessions	89
His Mastering Voice **Makes a First Appearance**	93
The Plays Resume...	95

    Boy
    Movers and Shakers
    The Buzz
    The Road

Falling Man
New Lover
Decisions
The Black Sheep
His Natural Life
The Lark
Windows
Lost and Found
Crashing and Crushing
Sidelined

Interruption!
His Mastering Voice Calls Out
from the Balconies   143
   Womans Business
   Half Baked
   The Mendicant
   The Formula
   The Wall
   Ship Shaping
   Back Again

Closing Scene
The Womans Sing the End   173

Encore!
The Mans Agree   175

Curtain Call
His Mastering Voice Wants
The Final Word   177

The Mans Have it
Men Must Change   179

End   181

The Dreamer Wakes   183

Found Much Later
Scrawled on a
Discarded Entry Ticket   185

Nocturnes: A Passage of Dreams

I.

Nocturnes is my witness to the pain of being human. As Freud spoke: "Life, as we find it, is too hard for us; it brings us too many pains, disappointments and impossible tasks". The dread that quietly prowls through our existence was captured by the German poet Walter Rheiner (1895–1925) when he exhaled: "I am human – I am afraid".

The wounding begins from our earliest years as the untainted child takes on the adulterations imposed by life. This drama is our human inheritance, a burden that must be borne as best we can. We cannot refuse to take it on but that won't stop us trying. Freud well knew our preference for denial. He went on to say that we employ various distractions so that we can bear the hurts and distresses that discolour our lives. Everything within reach is thrown at these wounds to salve them: gardening, art, professional ambition, commodities, children, narcotics, single malt, public ambition...just to start the list. For many of us, the daylight hours are consumed with the struggle to deny and turn back the tide of our species grief.

For we moderns, guilt is an extra freight; the price to pay for suppressing our natural instincts in favour of civilised society. We burn unconsciously with remorse, adding to our species pains. Philosopher Erich Fromm spoke of the "terrible burden of self-strength" that afflicts the enlightened, modern human, freed from the comforts of tradition and superstition. It is a constant and exhausting work to bear the afflictions – natural and self-made – that mark human life. Failure to acknowledge our hurts so often makes them much worse, usually without us realising why. Their hidden, unbidden work can corrupt our conscious lives in terrible ways.

And yet, as Freud offered, we can try to find means to live with these wounds without inflaming them. Various forms of therapy can lead us to this better place. The price is to let go of the comforting ruse of denial and accept that we are pained and painful creatures. We must go to therapists not exorcists because our wounds are an inseparable part of us. The promise is acceptance not resolution, consolation not cure.

Following Freud, when we sleep, these labours of carriage and denial are briefly quelled, and our griefs and guilts are freed to disport in the strange dramas we know as dreams. And of course, our buried desires join the throng, often with ribald song and forbidden play. In sleeptime, the heavily guarded prisons in our souls unearth the primal players who secretly animate our lives. I have called them the *Nocturnes. More on that later.*

We rarely speak much, and certainly not sensibly, about these dreamplays which consume a great portion of our lifetimes. A mattress salesman once advised me gravely to spend well on my purchase because "everyone forgets this is where they spend a third their lives". Imagine this arch commercial logic extended to the question of our emotional and psychic life? Regrettably, this seems indeed a work of imagination in the present day where dreams like death are inadmissible to public consciousness, at least in the Western sphere. Our dreamscapes are condemned to the margins of thought. We wake daily without arousing to awareness of our hidden lives.

II.

Nocturnes is my attempt to turn night into day, to bring to the stage of my consciousness the cryptic spectacles that are my dreams. It is the product of a time of severe emotional turmoil; the painful dissolution in early 2020 of a long-term romantic relationship amidst the wider unfolding calamity of the COVID pandemic. I say romantic with some uncertainty because this sentiment may express more wish than reality. In the wake of this passionate but turbulent coupling, it's still hard for me to discern what was truth, what was yearning, and what will always lie in the dark void of ambivalence that haunts every human relationship.

Nevertheless, the sudden and unexpected cessation of this long passion play took me by the throat and nearly extinguished my capacity to live. At this point the pain of being human, especially the part of it we call heartbreak, became too much, overwhelming all the defences that I usually employed as means to endure everyday life. The ordinary struggles were swept aside by this tempest. Capitulation to grief loomed like a dreadful thundercloud.

The turmoil brought a kind of fearful visceral clarity, roiling deep in the guts, aching across my chest. This great emotional backhander insisted I concede my fragile humanity. As well as emotional distress, I suffered illnesses of inflammation. The message from my body couldn't have been clearer – ignore me at your peril…our peril.

In fear for my collapsing life, I turned to my dreams because somewhere there my house was burning. I've described the dreamworld as a realm of existence that we rarely acknowledge but which holds our dearest feelings in blind trust. Hidden plays about secret things. Private screenings of our souls but in Dada not the language of our days. Freud established the basic means to investigate this hidden territory where the primal forms of our humanity roam. I had long pondered whether I would take the chance to follow his roadmap to the dreamworld, never knowing what would finally set me on it. The relationship crisis put me on the way of the dream pilgrim.

My dreams were fevered up by the hurt of the break with a generous extra contribution by the searing disruptions of the Covid outbreak in Melbourne, my homeplace. As with most other world cities, restrictions on movement were imposed by public authorities, but in Melbourne most harshly. For a long dark winter period, I was confined alone to my home, a small inner city flat, hostaged to my most basic psychic resources. And as I was to find out, captive to, and captivated by, the nocturnes that played up in my sleep.

Through a cold wet Winter into a hesitant Spring, we Melburnians endured the privations of strict lockdown. For my part, the long uncertain journey through the pandemic, and its public orders, felt like a passage that I had been suddenly forced into and through which I must make my way, alone. In this time, I felt subject to two opposing life (or death?) forces: simultaneously, blown up emotionally and harnessed physically. Things fell apart as the walls closed in. My body, my soul became ever more inflamed as the season grew wetter, colder. Reciting Freud I would say feverishly to myself, 'O Father I am burning'. And yet I quietly knew that I was talking to myself.

At one point, the daily delivered newspaper, a valued constancy, stated that people under the great confinement were dreaming furiously. Psychologists overwhelmed by eruption of human need reported this vast nocturnal gale. I knew this to be true in my own case, thrown nightly into realms of disturbed and disturbing sleep.

In the tunnel of lockdown, each uncertain day merged into each uncertain night. Increasingly I experienced the end of waking hours as the prelude, not to quiet sleep, but a night of restless, fatiguing dreamwork. I was especially plagued by disturbing, occasionally dreadful, dreams, some of which were long recurring reveries that I could put a quick name to, such as 'the scornful father', 'the wrong house' or 'the broken child'. At some point, I think in August, it occurred to me that the great disruption had lifted the lid from the hell of my repressed dreamworld. The Watcher on the Tower (Freud) had been driven back for a time – who knew for how long? – exposing the hidden fields of my emotional life. I knew I had to go there and meet my fate. There was gonna be a showdown.

This is, with the wile of hindsight, to summarise the protracted and ragged birth of a project of self realisation and survival that took the Wintertime to slowly rouse and form. In Spring, in the month of September, I began the work of recording and collecting my dream journeys, the project that became *Nocturnes*.

III.

Whence the name? It was an answer to the question: how to characterise the strange apparitions of dreams? I began with the idea of silent movies – discordant, enigmatic, and sometimes erotic – played out nightly in our dreams by a shifting cast of familiar and strange creatures. Dreams have always presented to me as a kind of paradoxical play: voiceless whilst soulfully scripted. A fitting established word for this seemed to be *Nocturnes*, or night music by night players. Here costumed in sometimes strange, sometimes ordinary garb were the guilts, hurts, and desires we are such poor hosts to.

In its infancy, *Nocturnes* was simply me wanting to record and thereby somehow quieten my fervid lockdown dreams. The first act of containment was to write them down, immediately upon waking. The method was simple, intuitive: to record only those dreams that cried out for capture in the moments of waking. This was to answer, when I could hear them, the siren calls of these nocturnes. My response was to transcribe them quickly into text, on my phone, usually in the partial light of dawn. They came out in verse form, and I never questioned why.

I have long had a poetic turning or yearning in my writing and this was awakened during the Covid dreamtime. The dreamscripts flowed easily, quickly in a poetic style that seemed both innate and new to me. In these intermittent poems dream spirits were caught and bottled, perhaps then to be undistilled and understood. Old hurts seemed to have been released by heartbreak. By respecting them, my soul might quieten, and my body cool down. The threat to my life might be averted.

As this work continued it became clearer to me that this was a project bound by time. A pilgrimage with an ending that would present itself when it was ready. Whilst I set out on a journey without knowing precisely when it would conclude, the 2020 calendar felt like a hard break. *Annus horribilis*, a year of living dangerously, with these *Nocturnes*. Somewhere near its end, my work would draw to a halt.

IV.

I started this testament by saying I believe that to be human is to be wounded. The hurts from our period of genesis may be so severe as to nurture in many hearts a secret desire for death, an extinction of pain, a return to the restful primordiality from which we were dragged kicking and screaming at the moment of conception. These deathly nocturnes enliven our dreams. Of course, Eros, our species duty to nature is there too, infusing (and confusing) our dreams with sensual plays that often break or upend the laws that govern our daylives. Dangerous violations of taboos abound. Eros and Thanatos, life and death, cavorting, but who will win out?

At this point, I should say that throughout the pilgrimage of *Nocturnes* I was accompanied by a wise and familiar guide, my therapist Elizabeth B. All wayfarers need, or at least crave, the comfort of guidance – the stars or a seer. In my case the latter, as Elizabeth B. helped me along the way during the hard, many times frightening, hours of this project. Following Melanie Klein, Elizabeth B. taught that all psychic roads start from the moment of conception. Gestation is thus potentially a vastly dramatic voyage, especially if the mothership doesn't want you aboard.

The truth, my truth, is that I was conceived and carried to birth as a desperate inconvenience by a teenage single mother in 1963–4. She did her best in this terrible situation, in an era of frightful conservatism, by bearing and delivering me to the world in secret circumstances. From there, good fortune took over and I was delivered as an orphan into the compassionate and yearning arms of my adopting parents, Brian and Mary. So began my warm upbringing.

Around the time I turned 21, Australian law began finally to allow adoptees to gain access to their birth records and origin stories. So it was that I learned about my birth parents, Elizabeth, and Terry. Their seemingly hard, early lives were the fountainheads of my own life. There was a lot of 'sturm und drang', as the Germans would say, in my early story. My passage to birth, carried by a young woman who had to dispose of me secretly without her family knowing, was an arduous road for all concerned. I was an affliction not a source of joy. As for so many others, the pain of being human was perhaps the earliest thing I consciously knew. In thrall to a callous adoption system, whose historical horrors are now finally well known, my mother suffered great emotional and physical privations so that 'the right thing' was done.

My adoptive parents, emotional geniuses for their era, told me from the first that I was given away by a "loving mummy who just couldn't keep me". I needed such consolation and my parents knew how to give it. There was, however, a deeply buried part of me that this story could not reach. There was a core of me that could not be consoled. I'll come back to that.

I recall that the telling of this creation story was left to mum but with father in the background, a quietly affirming co-signatory. My father had his own powerful way of claiming me, emotionally holding me to his chest as a real child. In a regularly repeated refrain through the years he described me as his 'number one son'. I felt that he meant it. After adopting me my parents had three children naturally, my sister and two brothers. I was thrown early out of nature's cradle, but this wondrous family caught me and tried their best to soothe my cries, put me on my feet for life. They had a lot of success.

V.

There is, however, no escaping the costs imposed by hard gestation and early separation. If I had exceptional fortune with biological parents who made me survive and adoptive parents who helped me thrive, my beginnings were nonetheless marked by a type of primal calamity that I share with many of my species. This is to be hard made and then torn out of the arms of the woman that bore you. To be misborn is to wear for life the invisible but timeless welts of 'the flogged wo/man'. Scars that bear testimony, acknowledged or otherwise, to the scourges of refusal and loss.

So, my two origin two stories sit at each end of a short scale of human possibilities: the hard start and the happy rebirth that followed. Put them together, in the right order, and you could say that I did well enough with my early life – and much that has followed. From the flames to the cradle, not the frying pan. This is the whole truth…if my deep birth scars are ignored. I think in my life I'd always swung back and forth between the narratives of boom and bust, love and neglect. In 2020, in contractions of grief, I was delivered to a more complex story.

VI.

In 1963, at the age of eighteen my mother, Elizabeth, left the family home in Perth with no one knowing that she was pregnant. It was a minor scandal that she chose not to finish her schooling. The nuns apparently were disappointed in the flight of this bright academic prospect who might have been Dux of the school. My mother showed independence and courage, even as she accepted hard authority and did the right thing. She went with a girlfriend to Sydney, a world away then, and worked, quietly waiting for my arrival. Elizabeth was a pious 'fallen' girl, who prayed regularly in a city chapel during her term, seeking the consolations of the French Saint for which it was named. In the last stage she was in Melbourne where I was born at the Royal Women's Hospital.

A birth certificate was rendered but through my early life, by law, I was never allowed it. This changed suddenly, sometime in my early twenties, when legislation was relaxed, and adoptees were granted permission to see their first testaments. Before this I was only allowed an 'Extract of Entry', which acknowledged my adoptive parents. It told the beautiful Christian (as it was then) name they had given me. My parents, Mary and Brian, later related stories of playfully debating that name, finally settling with my father's preference, an Irish Saint and adventurer. They fastened me into their joined history by giving me as middle name, my new paternal grandfather. Thus, I was made 'Brendan James GLEESON'. This was my extracted entry. I can now say, as I'm sure I always deeply knew, that this careful naming showed how my new parents accepted me and had hope for my life.

I recall the moment I first saw my birth certificate. It was passed to me, as a young man, by a public servant whose caring manner surprised me. She was no droll clerk. I'd earlier caught the train into Melbourne's city for this document handover appointment, vaguely aware by letter of invitation that it could contain 'new information' about my origins. This small official premonition didn't really register with me. I just expected to see my biological parents' names on something that confirmed my birth story.

Before passing the certificate to me, the kind woman asked if I was 'ok and ready' for it. I said yes and believed it. The protective confidence of youth. A light green facsimile of the original document was passed to me, and the first thing that struck was two very large stamps down the page, 'ADOPTED', 'ADOPTED'. Also was written in freehand on the right margin over its cold typed text, *'County Court Melbourne 30-8-66'*; presumably the moment in which I was finally passed through the adoption system.

I had not been ready for these black marks on my record. There were further surprises. First was to see in an official document my mother's name, 'Elizabeth Anne CONROY', who apparently lived at 'St. Joseph's Home, Broadmeadows'. The male parent was not named which was unexpected and concerning. I had grown up with a loving and attentive adoptive father. So, where was 'first Dad'? At the time I was unaware how routine it was to not answer that question in 1964.

With some discord, I scanned the rest of the green sheet. At the top (had I looked away at first?) I saw my certified birth name, 'Peter Julian CONROY'. "Who is he?", an inner voice immediately cried. That clouded question about my birth name followed me for a while afterwards, trailing soulfully behind. It was grey but also floating lightly. There was more wonder than sorrow in this surprising news. I wanted to know more about this lost me.

Sometime later, the mystery of this naming was clarified by my birth mother Elizabeth in our first meeting. This was when I learned the story of her Sydney pregnancy and of the holy Frenchman for whom I was named, Peter Julian. He who still hosts a handsome church in George Street, Sydney. Where, in a different era, troubled girls could sit quietly with a patient saint. No mansplaining, as we might say now. My mother found that place of solace in her time of exile, where the burden of me was eased for a time.

VII.

During this last year, when grief broke my heart open, a deeper significance of my first naming became apparent. It was a great revelation for my life. I believe that it came from the new empathy that suffering can grant you. My eyes, and my heart, were finally opened to the message that had long simmered in the birth certificate.

I said earlier that the 'mummy who loved me but couldn't keep me' story had softened my childhood. I had also quietly disbelieved this fairytale. As I grew older, and with more age and increasing distance from her, I hardened to the idea that my mother never wanted me. Even more, and perhaps difficult for you 'naturals' to understand, I believed that she saw me as an ugly misbegotten thing who needed to be cast out of her life. I was to blame for my greatest loss. From the beginning I carried this special guilt in a deep and inaccessible part of me.

After meeting my first mother as a young man, I tried to cast that fiendish story out of my soul. Indeed, following more reunions with her and my birth family, I really thought I had done it. The woman I met was a lovely ordinary human being whom I believed incapable of the malice that lay at the heart of my miscreation story. And yet, I now realise that the old blood written saga remained safely buried in my heart in the decades after this. It resurfaced in the turmoil of 2020 when female rejection returned to split my heaven and earth, again. Guilt visited like an old bad friend. She scorned what I secretly always knew. I was unloveable.

Elizabeth B. the analyst intervened, inviting me to reconsider my birth mother story. At one early point she offered, with a soft laugh, that my mother was a player not a slayer in the "psychodrama of your life". Clever work that gently lampooned my tendency to write history in Gothic font. A pictureshow followed in the therapy. In the first frame, the frightened schoolgirl that bore me for as long as she humanly could. Then we observed my next mother, Mary, the young woman who took me to a new manger where I would be loved, as I was, steadfastly, through my life. A good enough life followed. I saw it at last as an ordinary human drama not a horror story. It warranted an ordinary rating; at worst Adults Only but probably just Mature.

In a year cracked open by grief, a new origin story escaped to me. It follows.

VIII.

The one power my mother had in that terrible time for young women 'in trouble' was to give me a name for the official record. She was required to do this. Elizabeth applied a strong hand to the task. My first testament was a moment of human dominion, my mother pushing back against the great official will to nullify our primal relationship. We Catholics know what annulment means; the sanctioned dissolution of a consecrated vow. Conventionally this signified the ending of a marriage. I now think, however, that adoption, at the time, was another form of annulment – a virtuous way of ending a different wedding of fates. To deal with an impious problem: the birth of an unbearable child.

Today we often think of the termination of marriage as a disentanglement of names and narratives. The story of my annulment is very different. At the age of nineteen, as she let me go, my poor mother bequeathed me precious names that tied me to her family and her kind saint. She hoped that I would know this history one day and did something to make this possible. The birth certificate was her message in a bottle. A time capsule she threw to the seas of official censure with hope that it might one day drift my way. As it did.

In 2020, my heartbroken mind grasped this new creation story; a turning from the stock castaway tale of the adoptee. As the record stated, my mother's naming sought saintly blessing on me even as she removed me from her life. Strange names on a fading green piece of paper were benedictions not blows. For the first time in my life the word abandonment began with a small capital. For the first time I felt my mother's acceptance of me and her hope for my life. I relinquished the story of rejection. It was another fairytale.

IX.

No longer was I the homunculus of Goethe's Faust, a creature of alchemy not nature. I was human, not an exception to the species. Not so special after all. As Rheiner would know, my primal fears were a species condition not a personal curse. No creature had cast a bad spell on me. It was for me to decide what to do about my sufferings. I could succumb to them or I could try to live with them. My anguish cried for surrender but after a great painful act of will I rejected death. My beautiful children had provided my first line of defence. I've always known that I must be non-mortal for as long as they need me, until the time comes for change. I fed from that old spring and was back on my feet. But how to make the fight?

On which ground would I choose to make my stand? In what ring would I meet the grief monster? As a geographer, I thought about the question in terms of the time and space of my existence. Human life is a temporal journey through two great landscapes, day and night. At this time, my days were a prison of compulsive, straitened thinking; the same anguishes of loss on constant replay. It felt like a land of exhaustion – not a place to try and engage the enemy. When I thought about it further, harder, I realised that the blue feeling of each day was like that of a hangover. From what? I didn't have to think much to answer that question. I was daily wrung out by the hard fevered sleeps I was having. From nights of disport where it seemed a battle, *the battle*, was taking place.

So it was that I looked to my dreams. There I would venture in quest for my imperilled life. I was, however, no ordinary pilgrim; more like Flaubert's St. Anthony, making a terrible way beset by the demons of lust and death. It was a time of tears. Of silent weeping. If you read *Nocturnes* you will see what I mean by that.

X.

Nocturnes began in the Spring of 2020 and ended on the Christmas eve that followed. It is a sequence of forty-one dream poems that tells of a hard passage in my life. It was also the means through which I made and survived that hard journey, torn nightly by the demons of grief, and left to suffer their wounds quietly in painful days. This was a work of survival in a storm.

More than this, *Nocturnes* brought finally to the surface the stories of my mothers in my life, especially Elizabeth who had to discard me to ensure that we could both live. The question of human history was to the fore. This was in a year when our species seemed to be experiencing one of its horrible reversions. The human death drive seemed to be in overdrive. There was a pandemic of course, witnessing to the corruptions that mark our transactional relations with nature. We moderns had been there before with the Spanish flu epidemic, almost exactly a century before. A terrible scourge but things had eventually panned out. The cycle seemed vaguely reassuring; like the brief inundations safely predicted by 100-year flood maps.

This time, however, was darkened by the deepening shadows of political reaction (Trump, but so much more), the collapse of shared meaning (social media, but so much more) and continuing deterioration of the world's ecology. Looking back historically, it was as if, for us, the Spanish flu had been concertinaed with the decades of fascism and depression that had followed the outbreak of the disease in 1918. True, we didn't have global conflict or total economic collapse, but all this and more felt imminent.

We seemed to be in a time of great and possibly horrible change. In 1930, imprisoned Italian communist, Antonio Gramsci, sensing the rise of fascism in central Europe, told that "the old is dying and the new cannot be born; in this interregnum a great variety of morbid symptoms appear". He might have been writing of our terrible new times. The necessity of historical thinking was evident.

With morbidity everywhere making a claim, including possibly on my own life, the death spiral of Germany's Weimar Republic came to mind. As I began the work of dream capture, my thought was turned to the art and political expression of Germany in the early decades of the twentieth century. I suspected that this period and place of human history had a lot to tell me about loss and its consequences. It seemed a rich ground to go back to and learn from. Extending my limited knowledge of this world was an important means for occupying and quietening my troubled heart and mind.

The two new things worked together. The compelling work of capturing dreams as poems was accompanied and enriched by my labours, usually on the web each evening, to explore the premonitory griefs expressed in art and poetry as central Europe began to dissolve after World War One. For reasons I didn't need to understand at the time, I quietly knew that each labour depended on the other in the larger work that was *Nocturnes*.

Where to enter the vast German record of art and literature from that period, the first three decades of the twentieth century? The answer was not long in coming. In 2014 I published a book, *The Urban Condition*, which tried to think about our species situation now that we had become thoroughly urbanised. I chose for the cover an image of a 1925 painting by German artist, Conrad Felixmüller. It was labelled (in English) 'The Death of the Poet Walter Rheiner'. The painting depicts a suited man falling from a window towards a closely distant city, syringe in his left hand.

As a much younger man (I think it was 1988) I'd bought a print of this work in the Los Angeles Museum of Contemporary Art. The luminescent expressionism of the work appealed to my young romantic self. But I never made much effort to find out who Rheiner was. Years later, a few early perfunctory web searches went nowhere, and I let the trail go cold. The print was framed and placed on a wall wherever I lived in the decades afterwards. It always shimmered at me with some unspoken suggestion, but for what? Finally, in 2013 I thought I had the answer. It was the perfect cover for *The Urban Condition*, a dying human falling back into the indifferent embrace of the cities we have created (at least in the West). But I still had no idea who the falling man was.

As the *Nocturnes* journey began, the Weimar compulsion drew me back to Rheiner. After much investigation I found his story to be a remarkable, if terribly sad, one. Following hard and unwanted service in World War One he attempted a life of literature but was destroyed by drug addiction (and all that lies behind it), dying in 1925. Grief under the volcano of social change marks his work. I took to it and in 2020 gained a recent volume that has for the first time translated to English some of his many poems.

These were beautiful bent dream stories about human pain including in one the loss at an early age of his father. O Brother I've found you, I thought. Unlike you I must survive not succumb. But may I use your songs for a while? As September progressed, and my dream sequence unfolded, Rheiner's voice seemed to thread along like a wise, soulful narrator. Other such 'everyhuman' voices seemed to be emerging in the dream plays, wanting to be heard in the quiet writings of a desperate man.

Although artless, I yearned for images to evoke the main dream players. These were supplied by my discovery of the life and work of Heinrich Vogeler (1872–1942). I cannot recall how I found him in that dark-passaged time. Small wonder of late night searching and reading historical threads. Luck's a fortune, as they used to say.

Vogeler was two decades older than Walter Rheiner (born 1895), but both were middle class men from conservative backgrounds who served in the German army in World War One; experiences that deeply scarred each. Unlike Rheiner, Vogeler found a new life afterwards, as a dedicated socialist.

His previously romantic art and craft took on an entirely different, realist cast. Vogeler renounced his beautiful wife and daughters as well as his class privileges and went to live in the Soviet Union with the daughter of a Polish revolutionary and their child. The final story is a bitterly moving one, with Vogeler accepting exile and death in Kazakhstan in 1942.

As the Spring dreams flowed, I saturated myself in study of the work of these two men, and of the societies in which they made it. This looking up of history seemed as essential as the writing down of dream poems. The two labours converged to make something. A kind of play of poems came together in written and visual form. Over time, Central Players emerged to extol and shape the larger story that became *Nocturnes: A Passage of Dreams*. Deeply buried elements of my psyche and experience emerged to play their parts in a story about human griefs and their reckoning.

Rheiner rose from the grave to speak in the dream sequence through his sad poems. O, how I felt their common touch. He seemed to offer a collective male voice that I named, The Mans. Men would have been too sweeping, too wise. A century ago, Rheiner had captured the male experience as I had known it in my own life – just those mans of my story. Good human that he was, there came also from Rheiner's translated verse the voice of The Womans. Here I found parts of my female understanding drawn from the womans I have known in life and text. It amazed and moved me that this troubled soul could find time, before his early death, to see two sides of the human story.

Other players joined the cast that sang my dream sequence into a bigger story. My recently Lost Lover was first among them of course because she had abandoned me. This gave her star billing in my recent life drama. As it all progressed, I realised that our time together was yet another long and painful auditioning for the tale of loss. Late in the piece appeared His Mastering Voice, the voice of mature human reason that rose to speak in my life as I finally confronted these nocturnes. It's my prayer that he stays in my life.

XI.

Last year, when my world tore adrift from its moorings, I looked to dreams to find reality. This showed that my situation was dire. Grief threatened my life as a monster would. The choice was clear – fight for life or flight to death. After flirting with both I chose the former.

Like most of us I had always wondered about my night stories without going further to understand them. In a time of anguish, and the upending of normal things, they became the wild essential range of my (un)conscious life. This was where I had to go as wayfarer to encounter the spirits of hurt and desire that roiled within me. I knew I had to record their songs as a show of respect. To make a treaty with these primals. My hope, refined and encouraged by Elizabeth B., was that such work could bring me to safety in a time of peril. Even more, it might help me to finally live with these nocturnes. But I never got ahead of myself. First and foremost, I just needed to stay alive.

XII.

In 1964 my first mother Elizabeth Anne CONROY took me to the safe (enough) shores of adoption. It was a mighty act for a teenager to cross the cruel seas of Australian patriarchy at that time. My second mother Mary Mavis GLEESON was waiting to take me from her. She bore me a long way with great love. The courage of women. I learned it early on.

Of course, a painful rupturing lay below the surface of this good story. I was a handover, after all. The steadfast original mother was a deficit in my account. This quiet hurt was a long levy on my life. I was a misfooted boy never quite in step with normal things. There were consequences along the way of life. When I got things wrong with the Womans, which was regularly, the coin was always exacted with excruciating pain.

None of this destroyed me. I was taken up as an infant by sure stock who made strong children. It was a great endowment. I had means to meet my forfeits. Sometimes just enough, but always sufficient. So, my story is one of bad luck and good fortune. I am human. After all.

In 2020, I experienced the worst of Womans agony. This was the type of hurt that can kill me because it conjures, like a bad genie, the terrible drama of my original life. Not ready to die, I went to my dreamworld to parley with the enemy. I'd see if I could negotiate a truce with the angry spirits who had long taxed my soul with the misery of loss. I went to that place hoping to find my mothers to aid my quest only to realise I'd been carried there on their shields. Greatly moved by this discovery, I decided that it was time for me to repay their courage with a great fight. *Nocturnes* is my witness to that all-mighty struggle for life.

I hope this explains why I have dedicated this volume to my mothers, each of whom tried to ensure, in different ways, that I was well born(e). My creation grief is a hard legacy, but their love is a greater inheritance.

The Central Players

Lost Lover

Porträt Ilse Stoermer, Heinrich Vogeler, 1918

The Womans

Verkündigung, Heinrich Vogeler, 1901

The Mans

Sommerabend (Das Konzert), Heinrich Vogeler, 1905

The Dreamer

First love, again, Preparatory Class, Stella Maris

His Mastering Voice

Self-portrait, Heinrich Vogeler, 1900

Opening Scene, the Mans Speak

I am a human — I am afraid.
I fear the black clouds,
They: iron ringing on the dead border of the sky!
And I avoid house walls,
the silent doors frighten me;
sparkling handle, how fateful it touches my hand!

Overwhelmed by grey and shivering
soil, under God's cold blows and murderous stabs
– a human! What shadows of great, inevitable
           events!
I am afraid, I am terrified,
built, steered by the mystery word and magical line,
powerfully encircled by stars and storms and unfathomable
           one times one!

In the flash of the near sun at morning,
and in the bottomless gloaming of the portentous heart
I recognise myself and you, all of us, in our anguished being!
That which stalked us from the inception,
the creature, predator – God!, I feel revulsion!
How we are captured, buried and covered up by night
           and wind!..

Magical Song, Walter Rheiner

Dream Plays
September–December 2020

Arrow

Of all my ruined dream girls
My misbegotten children
You pushed
Into my heart
Hardest
Deepest

My broken tot
You disappear
You stray away

You don't speak
But I guess
At your moods

I went to find you
To bring you back
To that uncertain hearth
And the others
Who may
Or may not
Care
Meanwhile they watch
The busy painting
In the great room
Mute
With their
Little wonders

My heart was sore
For you
I remember you
My broken little doll

I found you outside
Vastly alone
Squatting
At motionless play
Your head removed

By your side
As you can do

I swept you up
Wishing you
Whole again
Fearing
A losing cause

Hard clasped
I took you inside
You must eat
Little girl creature
Never nourished

I pleaded for you
With the silent ones
Who bear
No intercession
You are the unseen
Little end of us
Who goes
Her own way
Must do

I brought your face
To mine
And saw you were ruined
Around the eyes and cheeks
Two continents
Of crocodile skin
You were silent
With my anguish
At your pest face

The bolt moved hard
In my heart
As I held you close
Unable to help
I must find you
A salve

Arrow
My lost little ruin
My child
My charge
My fault
You draw my love
Freely and deeply
It rushes out
As from a wound
To a squandered place

I hold you
Broken and pestilent
To my sore chest
I stand with you alone
By the precipice
By the vast tableau
I have found you
You are safe for now
But all is lost

(Dream date: 17 September 2020)

She Moved On

Sleep
And you may dream
Of loss
Until
Released at dawn
From griefs
By roaring street cleaners

This city has a claim
On everything
Even dreams
Especially mine

I wandered
Through the
Bright angular night
Of the dreamworld
Along its hard trigonometry
Looking for you lost lover
Always a step ahead
And behind you
They said you had just left
And that you might arrive
Sometime unknown
I sent messages
To your silent mind
But you had moved
Out of range

I think I heard you say
My name
But it fainted
Across the great divide
Only a murmur reached me
By then it was more
Rumour
Than word
Or was it just
My sigh

I knew there was
No end
To this
Hard journey
Always leaving
And never arriving
With heavy slurried steps
Talking to you through myself
Like a madman
On his
Staggering
Muttering
Beseeching
Way

Until freed from purgatory
By droll machines
Wrenched
From the dream
To lose you
Further
Deeper
Harder
In the void of day

(Dream date: 22 September 2020)

The Wronged House

I can be uprooted
A long way to a place
Where I cannot recall
My home
Or even if I have one
For a while
I'm where it seems
I must be
On the hard margins
With nothing but
Gut instinct
And my
Brothel creeping shoes

In my farthest house
There are many rooms
Wrong and ruined
Serried
Twisted
Rubbished
Accumulations of
Ambition
Spite
Neglect
Well mostly mindlessness
The many perpetrations
Of scrupulous wasters
Who built hard
Only to deem this spoil
And vanish

I am mustered here
By musts
Must fix these
Many messes
Must get these houses
In order
Journeyed hard to get here
Or did I just appear

From afar
On a long string

Must be about
This farthy business
There is only me to do it
It seems

Inertia roils in
As a clear sapping fog
I'm bled away
Through missing boards
And tiles
Into the black dusted cavities
Below
Towards those secret
Rumoured voids

This is not the only
Problem
Rooms refuse
The readying hand
Their rubbishes scream
Defiance
At arrangement
Their moulds ooze
Stubborn
Despondent

And there's manslaughter
Of bad geometry
Afoot
In off beamed parlours
And faithless passages
That never quite connect
And what about
Those sleazes
In the air
Defilements
A peace that dreams
To be disturbed

Everything is aggrieved
But not yet ready
For grief
For moving on
And you are torpored
By that

It takes more courage
Than you think you have
To rouse
Vanquished again
By the wronged house

(Dream date: 24 September 2020)

The Black Sun

Father I'm burning
Torched by your scorn

You see me to scald me
Your eyes are solar flares
Warning the world
Of my travesties
Your mouth
A sneering rictus
Seething holy fires
On me

You walk me
By the scruff
With your gaoler's stare
To the liturgy of account
Where I will be
Unnamed
The last time

We press
Along the snarling way
Until suddenly
You are gone

Without you father
I'm unreckoned
Not worthy it seems
Of your ires
Your fires
For all you care
I can walk to judgement
Alone

I am burning hard now
With your biled gift
A red green scald
Inside me

Woe
To the misbegotten child
Who will not face
The confessor

Father
You are justice
You are law
The awful incandescence
Of truth
I look up to you
You lord
The uncertain sky

You are the black sun

(Dream date: 25 September 2020)

Transgressions

I sit accused
At a dealer's table
Reposed
After some half-known
Deeds
Did I really

The dream confessor asks
Is this what he's been
Doing
All day
In Melbourne

My small confederacy
Has fled
Youngish women
We'd best not call girls

She has more to say
You'd been warned
We'd caught you at it
Several times

The great green lady
Old and young
Looking down
A beaked nose
Appears and
Disappears

But it's not over yet
Not by any means

It's coming

I wake
Impatient for penance
Let's get this
Over with

(Dream date: 27 September 2020)

Global Sequence

I. German house

I'm lying amidst
Child's play
Stomach flattened floored
The mother has been talking
To me
She has placed herself
On my back
Settled onto me
I feel her pubis
On my lower portion
Pushing into me
Just above my tail bone

She's lilting my ear
But what is this
Other message
Soft grinded below
I feel her short hair
The patch of her
She may be making
A point

Earlier I'd met hubby
He hadn't liked me much
Or perhaps not even cared
Went off for business
In a sports car
Vroom

I'm pinned down
But moved
By this ambush
By this bush
Public private intimacy
I know what's going on
Even if no one else does
He'll return

But isn't here now
During the conspiracy

The mother speaks
Of her children
As they play around us
Two more are on the way
All the while
The decadence of her
On my back
And yes
That point of pressure
Do I feel pleasure
Or just gratitude

Next I'm walking nearby
Released from the house
My departed law mother
Is on the road
Decreeing
Ask the husband
For money
A lot of money
A donation for your cause
He and the wife
Are wealthy

I must do this
At the lunch
That's all arranged
For soon at the house
I must go back
Must I really
Wasn't warned
I'm not easy for it

I return to the house
Which becomes a mess
More than
The little disarrays
Of children

Now it's all
Unfolding disorder
Across rooms
With adults involved

My daughter is there
But she is having
None of me
Won't speak

Shimmering vexation
And
Another journey
Starts out from here
This is another story

II. The other story

I leave the house
Its sideshows
I'm leaning towards Asia
It's probably Japan
Which makes sense
From Germany
A long train journey
To a city for
The next thing
In company of cardboard others
Suddenly we're stopped
Everyone must alight
This is not straightforward
I'd travelled separately
From the others
The cutouts
In the carriage behind
Now I must recover my bag
In all this haste
A melee of exits

At this point
My daughter appears
Her impatient voice
Is pulling me
By the hand
Away from my heavy feet
I'm fretting over loss
Of things and connections
And she's lecturing me
On ecology
It's the water on the train
That matters
She says
Each train must have
Enough
That's the real point
Enough water
Not stolen luggage
She reprimands

I counter
You go and get that bike
I promised you
She fades away

I'm trapped
Slow frantically looking for
Lost luggage
In overhead lockers
I'd trusted
My black briefcase
To the company
I'd left it forward
In their locker
Foolish me it dawns
Slowly but not surely
The last people are departing
The company is vanished
They know
What they're doing.
And when to do it

All change
Is the cry
I didn't change
In time

Any moment
A carriage jolt
Forwards to what is
Surely coming
But not the end of the line

Orphaned luggages
Are on the floor
Some spilling their guts
It's all a bit of a mess
I will miss my connection
To the speedy train
My head fast forwards to it
I can see it's
Not so speedy
After all
My body slurs
In the stopped train
That is threatening
Any moment
To move
To kidnap me

The departure lights
The warning signals
Are on
I'm hostaged
How will this end

It ends
At about 7.30 am

I'm on my back
That bore the mother
For a while

Should I sleep on
Captived to the train
No I must stir to recall
The message
In the mother's tongue
That secret undeciphered
Has stayed with me
I'm still surprised
And yes
A little pleased

I write back
Thankful for her crime
And the rare gift
Of a good beginning
To a day

It's a happy man that lies
With a sinner
Who knows how to press
Her claim

(Dream date: 28 September 2020)

Tempus Fugitives

I squeezed my car without roof
Or sides
Along a walkway
A passage
Far up a tall building
You should be able
To get through this
There were passenger lifts
At either end
And somehow the car would
Fit in later
So you could go all the way
To the ground floor
And onwards wherever

But all that lay ahead
In my head
As I travelled along
The roofless hallway
On an upper floor

In the middle was a choker
That some infernal builder
Had decided to throw
Into the bargain
It also marked an opening
To the right
John Wiseman
My old colleague
Was sitting next to me
It wasn't clear
Who was steering
Because there was no wheel
Then we hit that squeezer part
And it was me
Getting us through
I'd done this before
Could do it and explain it
In our shared thinking

Amazingly we got around it
But everyone does with a
Little bending and effort
And it helps to drive an air car
In these situations

We squeezed through
And I was awake

Earlier I felt surprised
By the passing of time
In these journeys
How much could go
Without you noticing
It was like
A ringing of bells
In fact it was
A ringing of bells
You listen to them
Not realising those tricksters
Are stealing your watch

I caught this thought
Inside the dream
And promised to take it
With me
To the other side
It made me impatient to get to
The other side
Whilst I could still hold it

Next thing I knew
I was in the passage

(Dream date: 4 October 2020)

A Drop Off

The scornful father
Paid a visit
In a swarthy skin

He dropped me off
Well really dumped me
From the car
In front of the wife
And kids
For all he cared
I could walk

I decided I could
I knew the way
Along the windy coast road
I knew where that husband
Was driving
I knew as well as he did

Since writing my letter to him
A few weeks ago
He seems to have lost some of my
Respect

(Dream date: 4 October 2020)

One Act One Play

I was on her
Working away
Upwards
But it was faltering
With fallouts
And restarts
I was deeply arriving
To no reception
Shown the door each time
Only to return
With grim determination
Surely at some point
She'd let me stay
Or at least let me
Get there

It was starting to go on
A bit
As she minded to me
And no release was
In sight

I knew her
With that girlish boyish face
From an earlier time
When I had tried to be
Her lover
Without much success
We'd have to say

I breathed into her ear
Oh I wish we'd done this
Properly
Back then
At the right time

She simpered doubtfully
We were out of time

All the while
People came and went
In the open room
A passing teacher
Tried to hide our sight
From his children

Then a woman arrived
And folded up our act
For transport elsewhere
Where it would be displayed
We were going to the circus
The show
We'd escaped from
To make this private play
She hadn't been convinced
At the time

Does it always have to end
This way
With us

(Dream date: 8 October 2020)

The Beanstalk

My son was sniffling
And asked for a tissue
Do you have one

The getting of it
Required climbing
A giant tower
Up a long terrible
Enclosed ladder
That was clinging to its side
Has anyone tried this
Recently
Without falling back to earth

I decided to get up
For a piss
Instead
It was better
For all concerned

The tower had dominated
A long dream sequence
It was good to be shot of it
Something had to change

(Dream date: 13 October 2020)

Nightwatchmen

I was having a few beers
With Pat Fensham
We were in a room
Full of jumble
Somewhere inside the University
Pat seems to know his way
Around
This part
Better than me
He'd brought chairs
And we were looking at them
Family heirlooms
Wood, patterned, straightbacked,
Not comfortable
His father could advise
Their provenance

His family were donating
The chairs
To the University
It seemed a strange thing to do
But then again
These things happen at night
And I said mate
It's alright
They'll take anything
These days
Even fake turf

There wasn't much to do
Except decide whether to have
Another beer
Some odd fellow
Was coming and going
In the background
Was it Pat's crafty brother
Otherwise all was quiet

I think we were waiting
For dawn
I was getting a bit impatient
For it
Sometimes these stories
Drag on
And you know that
Even inside the dream

There were things to do
The coming day
The actual coming day
Which added
To the pressure

Pat had plans too
We were both a bit
Preoccupied
But at least
There was beer
Would we have
Another one
He seemed a bit
Concerned
By the question
Not me

(Dream date: 13 October 2020)

Flight of Fancy

Last night I realised I could fly
Well hover
Just above the ground
With my invisible air pack
And move along
With a slight tilt leftways
Pretty smooth stuff

I took myself
For a test run
To the toilets
Arriving smartly at a long urinal
I put myself down
Very well
I landed
In the right place

Meanwhile
I was at a gathering
Of political economists
Naturally Frank Stilwell was there
They were doing their weekly
TV broadcast
To a world that should be
Concerned
They were always trying
To get through
To deaf ears
The big chiefs
Were taking turns
I looked down
From the balcony
And saw the main orator
Schlepping through
The gathering
I caught and dropped
His strange little name
Moe was it
Hey Moe
Mo hoper

Up here in the balconies
I wasn't
Completely convinced

A well regarded fellow
Showed me a script
For his segment coming up
It wasn't English
I could recognise
He seemed to be writing
To himself
Maybe he just needed
To be regarded
Or guarded

Jago Dodson turned up
With a tic
That proved to be quite
A distraction

The story diverted
For a while
To the question of bodies
I gave Jago
A bit of a talking to
About his condition
He went off to a cubicle
To have a think about it

All the while I realised
I should have been paying
Attention
To the weekly show
Watching the segments

But that shaking friend
Had needed my attention
A wake up call

And that little flying expedition
Seemed

Pretty important
Surely they'd be impressed
It was a breakthrough
After all
At least for me

Or was it just tommyrot

It was hard to say
Right up to the end

(Dream date: 14 October 2020)

Unreeled

I was in a video call
Up against the screen
Hard at it
Talking to a university
Honcho
A Pro Vice Chancellor
PVC
Plastique
A blower
Upper
Maybe

Big things were happening
Far away
The grandee was staying
At the Marriott in Bangkok
Sounded like a hotspot
Something important
Had happened
But what

Meanwhile little things
Were happening
Around me
Distracting me from Bangkok
My two kids
Were hustling me
For attention
Right up close
Julian was about
Seven years old
And Alison was
Well younger of course
These bumble bees
Distracted me
And I bumbled
The PVC
Oh dear

I arced up
Shooed the kids away
They were both upset
Julian needed to pour himself
A whiskey
He produced two
One in a dangerous long glass
With chipped razor lip

Heaven knows where Alison
Had gotten to
With her good sense
Her brother sulked off
Somewhere
With his sharp dram

It was all a bit of a muddle
Bangkok can't be happy
And what was that event
I'd missed
Or
Misheard

I woke
Wishing I'd been nicer
To the kids
To my littlies
Oh Julian that glass

(Dream date: 15 October 2020)

Walking the Line

I was running across
A lot of train tracks
At a huge station
An interchange
Bare as a baby's bum
Trying not to get run over
Then I was in a car
With a woman I should know

We crossed to the other side
I found a car park
By a platform
On a line that would take us
Where we needed to go
It was a crafty park
Usually reserved for railway staff
On the inside of everything
I gave myself a pat
On the back

Pulling up we discussed
The workshop
That lay ahead
A public meeting
To debate cutting red tape
It was to be chaired by
A well known cutter
She'd come over from
The other side
I was on the panel
I hoped I'd have
Some clothes on
By then
And also time for a wee
Before

That chairwoman
Doesn't she have a conflict
Of interest

I asked the driver
Oh no
She'll make it all work
Was the reply
You'll see
It's what women can do
On a good day

We got out and walked
Towards the platform
I was really needing
The loo
Now
Could I hold on
It wasn't a long journey
But a bit dicey

I was looking for bushes
When a train pulled up
The crowd surged forward
And my companion rushed in
And shut the door
Behind her
I was struggling with the door
Lots of people were

The train lurched off
A gasp from the many
Who didn't get in
We'd missed it
Then it halted
As if to let us on
After all
But didn't
Off it went
Tricksy driver
Probably under orders
So what's the point

For my small part
It was a relief

I still needed a wazzer
It was one of those
Rare platforms
With toilets
The woman's were handy
The man's were not
A sign advised all women
It would take your man
7 minutes to reach it
It had a strange picture
Of a gnarly old man
With a walking cane
God
Are we all that hopeless
I thought
This was getting
Exhausting

Then relief came
Without the walk
The noisy builders
Across the road
Had started early
And got me
Up and out of there
I still had no clothes on

(Dream date: 16 October 2020)

Doing Time

Dublin
I was staying with
A family
I vaguely knew
Waiting to leave
The country
I wanted to go home

Mother was pretty
Put out
Tired
I was another mouth
To feed
A big one
Some social things
Happened
Without me
I wasn't evicted
But also
Not really wanted

I can do this I thought
I rolled my sleeves up
And did the dishes
To help out
To try and please her
Rolling my rock
Up her hill

She was all sighs
And heavy steps
Off to see about
The little ones

I decided I can't do this
Must leave and go
To a hotel
For the last few days
But that would have to be

Tomorrow
How to endure
Another day
How would the night
Work
I was doing time

Mind you
Father said
With his general's hat on
That man goes hard at it
He'd be handy
In an invasion
Of the Iberian Peninsula
Or even
A whole campaign

That was something
At least
I woke
With a strong erection

(Dream date: 17 October 2020)

The Womans

I met the womans
Of my dreams
Last night
Twice
She came
With a family of visitors
The older daughter

At first she was swarthy
Bug eyed
And libidinous
She said
We were going to do
It
Oh hah we sure were
And laughed
Like a pirate
I was getting worried
This was not for me

Fade
And some other
Sequences
With those visitors

Then she was back again
As a comely gal
Visiting from next door
Same family
Bit beaky but cool

She also said
We were going to do
It
This time I thought
Fine

Now she was the one
To worry

Asked
Will you make
A mess and noise
I felt I could give
The wrong answer
I faltered
She said
None of that stuff
Will be necessary
Because
We'll already have
A connection

I thought
Well aren't you
The careful miss

I looked at her
She was nice enough
No oil painting
Except that she was
I'd seen her hanging
Somewhere
Favourable

You'll do I thought
I pulled her to me
And put my arm around
Her neck
We started to walk
Towards that adventure
But then
We both disappeared

An hour awake
And I still think it's a pity

(Dream date: 17 October 2020)

The Fool

England
I think I'm staying
With Phil and Jen
But where was Jen
Other friends were coming
Including
Steve from Follyfoot

I find myself examining
A poorly made municipal fence
Crappy
Brown
Wooden
It was a temporary
Shingled thing
To section off some
Deadish space
That people needed
To stay out of

I wasn't convinced or happy
And decided to consult
Passersby
My friends were
Disinterested
Couldn't care
More or less

Up comes a couple
He was a large
Plodding
Man
She was silent
And seemingly distressed
They were clearly
Party animals
And drugged
Off their tits
All of them

He jumps the fence
And takes her with him
He ends up flat on his face
An embarrassing show off
But this is worrying as well
He has
Lots of force and energy

What about her poor thing
Well she was useless
Or maybe just helpless
Let's give her
The benefit of doubt
Which really means
Ignore her
If you're honest

Also the gal turned into
A younger male
For a while
A sidekick
For the big clown

I'm stuck with him
And maybe her
Since it was me that decided
On the public consultation
He's addled
And I must put up with
His nonsense
There's a vague threat
In the air
But I decide to err
On the side of him
Just being an idiot

We have an idiotic conversation
As I try to bring him around
He also tries to bring himself
Around
Showoff

My friends have retreated
If they were ever there
Back to the house
For refreshments
And a film

Steve appears later
Asks me and the lout to look
For the movie cylinder
That had been on its way
Before all this nonsense
Happened
I rummage through
The druggie's mess
But no cigar
I'm not impressed
Just want this resolved

I retreat to the house
Which has no walls
Or roof
The usual
Stage
I'm keen for a beer
And a break
Friends are coming and going
In the background
But of course they're all
More voice than body
All talk
You'd have to say

I'm looking for a beer
In the mini fridge
There's an assortment
Of unappetising types
For god sake this is England
We can do better
Who's going
To the off-licence
Not me
I'm stuck here

On the spot
Peering into it

A daft acquaintance
Makes a point of saying
He's not drinking
Alcohol
Tonight
A bit of a shameman
I take the bait and say
I wouldn't either
If this is a Monday
Or Tuesday
Not really believing myself

I can see soft drinks
In the fridge
Nothing's happening
Then I spy a card
From the oaf
Amongst the cans
Was it a thank you
For all our efforts
No just a brash
I was here
Boor
Beer
Boor

Then things get strange
And interesting

The girl is being treated
By some friendly strangers
Experts
She has a slice
A kind of scarry wound
On her upper back
Right shoulder blade
The cosmetic medicals
Are working on it

Cold sore cream
Will do the trick
And is applied
Or will be
It will swell the lips
Or maybe shrink them
Hopefully bring them back
Together
And give her a break

I doubt it will work
Poor lass
But it's their thought
That counts
Off she goes
With the pros
Good riddance
I mean that goodly
As well as riddly

All this work
With the public
Is
Exhausting
Why do I insist on doing it
I ask
I can't seem to
Help myself
Not even to a beer
That still hasn't happened
Yet

I wake then very thirsty
And reach for the water glass
Glad to be free of the fool
Not sure I've learned
My lesson

(Dream Date: 18 October 2020)

She Rules

Lost lover was there
And abouts
In the night stories

At one point
She made a cold
Little theatre
For me
Cooing over an infant
Probably a nephew
Nurturing it in
A boxed cradle

There was some point
To be made
But it passed by quickly
And I didn't really catch it

She said about her children
I give them all the first
Twenty years
That's my starter gift
She didn't have to convince
Me
I know
What they are in for
What they can expect

Meanwhile
We were fast careering
Towards a splay of kids
Playing on the road ahead
We'd clean them all up
If she didn't look up
Pay attention

We needed to change
Course
She was prepared to play

Chicken
Because she could
Ruled the roost
Always did

Oh look out kids
Here we come

Caring
Careering
Not caring
That was her way
My heart went out
For her
And all the children
But I knew I'd have to
Choose

Too late
I woke
So chest sore
For the day

She'd been coming
And going
In the dream
Sequence
Playing my heart strings
With her talons

(Dream date: 19 October 2020)

Second Dream Sequence

The Decision

I'm lying in the half light
Called awake by nature
This matter had been
Under discussion
Just now in my dream
Would I go through with
It
A question mark
Was hanging
Over my head

There was a weighty matter
In the dream as well
Now lost in the works
Something to be realised
If I was to move to
The next stage
What was it
It might have had
A number on it

I'd been giving myself
A bit of a talking to
That extra voice of mine
Was there
Mastering
And the issue of
Getting up
For relief
Was central
To the conversation

My bladder was there
Arms crossed
A cocked eye
Tapping its foot
To press the point

Someone had to decide
Had to act

It's 7:02
Melbourne October
It's not dark or light
I haven't gotten up
I'm not convinced
By myselves
Including
That foot tapper

I could go back to sleep
But I'm not sure
I'd get a good
Reception
Until this is sorted out
I'll drink the water
Next to me
A delaying action
It might make things
Worse

Out of my hands

I got up
Did the necessary
A done deed done
And went quickly back
To sleep
Welcomed
With open arms
Well swallowed up
Quickly

I busied myself
At a workbench
In a roofless shed
Knowing I was expected
For a plane trip
To Bali

For some conference
I knew little about

The more I thought about it
I knew nothing about it
I packed carefully
Not realising how
Half hearted
I was about it
This became clear
Later

A colleague
I don't much care for
I could put it more harshly
Came to advise me
On this mysterious show
It would be ok
He assured
One worthy thing
Was going on
A good design
By masters students

I was far from convinced
Seemed like
Middling little masters
At least he wasn't such a prat
For a change
But students were all he could
Resort to
Typical

We were expected
To meet the pilot
To check in with her
This lady in drab green
With an unconvincing hat
It felt like an interview
I was first up
I had nothing to report

Or ask
She sighed
Disappointed
And left to walk alongside
The outside
Of the plane
It was a mile long
But I knew we'd all be
Squashed inside

Back to packing
And a rising mild panic
The more I thought about it
The more essential things I knew
I hadn't bothered to bring
No footwear
For heaven's sake
And that was just
The start of it

It was probably all too late
The case was full
And shut
My eyes went briefly
Inside it
And couldn't see any room
I wouldn't get a shoe in

I thought about being
In the air
In that squishy plane
It was not appealing

My brother briefly
Threaded around
He grounded me for a bit
But was too fast
Flitted away

The time for departure
Was probably coming

It would arrive
Like a thief
In the night
The thought hung over me
With a foggy menace
I was worried
But also cross
With myselves
Or someone
For getting me into
This

Why this
Why me
Everyone knows
How much I hate flying
These days
There was a time I loved it
But that has long passed

Time
It's not in my hands
It's running through
My fingers
But one thing was clear
One day I'd have to
Take that flight
With the drab captain
And there's no way
I'd be ready
The situation was probably
Unsalvageable

(Dream date: 20 October 2020)

Performances

I. Showman

A modest music jamboree
It had followed
A dream
About bank clerks
My own history as one
So things were getting
More upbeat
And at last
The bands were
Playing

There probably was
An actual audience
Not just me
The dreamer
Am I

I'm talking about
Those air beings
You can feel them
Hold their moods
But you can't see them

An older fellow was key
To the whole thing
A sliver eminence
He was holding
The program
Together
When it came time
For his act
The invisible crowd
Who now seemed to be
One person
Called out for more
Play it again Sam
Because they hadn't

Got him
The first time

I was off stage
But close behind him
And thought
You crafty shyster
You're actually
A conductor
Disguised as a player
No fool
Like an old fool
But another part of me
Applauded
His gall

From the wings
I thought
We seem to be stuck
With ageing troubadours
These days
But here at least
Was one
Trying

Nonetheless
The moral of the story
Seemed to be
That despite
The lofty claims
Of art
It's really always about
Ourselves
And besides
This concert
Was going
Nowhere

The whole thing
Was a step up
From the earlier dream

With me
As a frustrated bank boy
My older self
Was telling the story
Of me
As a young fool
I was trying
To get through
To the audience
The doubtful stalls
With a droll tale

So when it came
To the concert
I could give myself
A break
By then I was critic
Not composer
Who could go along
For the ride

Then
In the dark
Quarter awake
I thought
These silverbacks keep
Popping up
Somebody clearly
Must keep an eye
On them
A critical lens
But it won't stop them
They must be heard

I can still see
The not so great
Pretender
In the middle of things
Holding it together
Holding it up

The show must go on

II. The Dead Horse

I return to sleep
Back to that domain
To the slope
Which was
Another part of it
I'm walking down it
Lost lover is below
I plan to cry
Before her
Let it all hang out
But then decide
No I will
Harden up

I wake that way
Good I think
It's a stiff situation

And I say to myself a
Aloud in the dark
I'm flogging
A dead horse
But why

III. The Flogged Man

I sleep again
She's back
This time she's
Much closer
Staying in my room
In another bed
Empty
And
Unmade

She's out for the day
And maybe the night
On the town

My heart sinks
Even lower
I pick up a ball
Of her cast off hair
And smell it
But it's scent less

She returns
To argue a point
About Baudelaire's grammar
She's critical of him
Of a title sentence
Dismissive
Smarty pants

I tell her
I used the same start
As Baudie
In my project
A Passage of Dreams
That's it
I've let my guard down
Given my game away
Up for her grabs
Right inside
The dream

I've lost
Loser
Flogged man
The scars
On the back
Of
My
Heart
Ache

I wake again
It's still dark
But dawn is coming
Please

IV. The Other Voice

I nod off briefly
One last time
I ask myself
Do you want
To write this
Down
To my surprise
I answer myself
With a firm
No

(Dream date: 24 October 2020)

Dream with a Chaser

I. Airhead

I was packing
The family camper
For the return trip
Home
Busy body me
Standing up in it

Then I spied a flying boat
Coming towards us
It was an aluminum dinghy
With a glassy shed on top
A tinnie plane
With a propeller
Out the back
The driver was a silhouette
It was heading
Downwards
Oh no I thought
I hope it doesn't come to me
I don't need the company
Of that airboat
And its impudent driver

The pilot swooped lower
Would he fly onwards
I turned away
So he couldn't
Catch my eye

Of course
It landed next to our van
And the boat became
A shed on the ground
Out spilled a mess
Of youngsters
Who got busy
With organised play

All had vaguely familiar faces
Were they children
Of people
I knew
Or the actual people
I couldn't recall
Any of their names
It was possible
That we were all related
They had knowing looks
Slightly rueful looks
How would I know
Their names
When it finally came time
For us all
To speak

I pondered this situation
Perhaps I'd ask them to
Introduce
Themselves
To me and my family
Give in you dreamer
I said silently
To my head
Just say you failed
From the first
Get a small act
Of discourtesy
Out of the way
So we could move
On
Then the proper talk
Could begin

There was another problem
A compounding one
I had an erection
A hangover
From sexy thoughts
Earlier in the dream

Another scene
On the holiday
The truly illicit part
It took work to hide
The extruder
And it kept popping out of
My trousers
Godsake
This is no way to go about
Things
Very
Bothersome

Back to the first
Dilemma
I was talking with the pilot
Or trying to
My couple of kids
Had showed up
From the motel room
Were they just part
Of the holiday troupe
Chubby imps
Watching and grinning
From the roof
Of the camper
A show was about to happen
I was the teller
But stuck for words
It was a hard situation
Like all the others
Before

Tight corners
They just keep coming
At me
Flying at me
Who else gets hunted down
By pesky airboats
Full of childish expectation

I turned down the role
Solved the problem
By turning it off
Woke
Not proud
But not
Ashamed

II. A Royal Mess

I returned to sleep for a while
Back to Royal Park
Where I'd been
The day before
To the illegal bike jump
Made by naughty boys
Who couldn't give
A toss
I turned to lost lover
And asked
Is your boy part of this
Mischief

Good grief
Who was I talking to
I started
Panicked
Realising we were still
On speaking terms
I had to get out of
There
So I ditched
The whole dream
For the daylight
Like a coward
A lucky one

(Dream date: 25 October 2020)

Intercessions

Abschied, Heinrich Vogeler, 1898

The Womans Respond

...And she replied, singing: 'I don't know you anymore, Olaf, my love.
Look, I sit in the arbour and the moon casts singing nets.
And my soul is with you above the roofs of the great city.
Your step a high cantilena, Olaf, my thou,
my heart wandering outside.
Behold, how the night effloresces my eyes.
Ah, they drain the sky, meeting you.
And your last hand-kiss is a slow dance on this snow of your hand, Olaf.
We fall asleep at the same time, our souls fall asleep.
Where do our bodies lie, separated or close or far?
We are intertwined,
and the world is a pearl musical box in our breast,
around which the nocturnal winds blow...'
She startles, her face exceedingly bright;
it falls from the sky,
a moonstone.

Three Fragments from a War Novella, Walter Rheiner

Then the Mans Have a Say

We traversed all foreign cities
and distance radiates from our coats.
The buildings burn palely into our skin.
Trees and street lights, entangled twisted thorns
around our blue and star-enveloped brains...

Are we rotting? The night is always there!
Sweetly we sink in nameless velveteen.
Already our shadows haunt the rooftops.
A grey and pointless day knocks on the window.

The moon, this yellow eye stares upon us
and moans back and forth like a carnivore:
the people, hypnotically entwined
with it, hang out from chimneys, corpse-like.

Embellishments creep through our dead bodies,
from a woman who possesses our souls...

Dreamt images take flight with cries...

And the Nile streams great into our hearts.
Now we are sea, are sand, are hazy stars.
The earth continues, the pale ball floats up there.
We are substance and ether. Who forms us?

Night and Dream, Walter Rheiner

His Mastering Voice
Makes a First Appearance

To become properly acquainted with a truth,
we must first have disbelieved it, and disputed against it.
Sleep is for the inhabitants of planets only. In another time,
Man will sleep and wake continually at once...

Fragments, per Thomas Carlyle, 'Novalis' (Georg Philipp Friedrich von Hardenberg 1772–1801)

The Plays Resume...

Boy

I was at a mass
Gathering
In India
And you know
How they do
Mass
There
Massive

People were pouring
In for the show
Towards the centre
With important speakers
A religious overtone
Local custom stuff
Important
Impressive
Rousing
Everyone from afar
And me

I saw a white
Missionary priest
On the way in
His nephews had turned up
And he urged
Respect
For the masses
We were outsiders
In the human flow

I followed a gaggle
Of interesting women
Locals insiders
One Amazonian was destined
To make a show
Of things
We found a good perch
Under trees

Behind the speakers
Or they did
Crafty gals

The Amazon
Was causing a stir
Approaching
The speaking circle
Bare breasted
The elders weren't impressed
She was determined
To make her points

By now
Everyone was becoming
More European
And less Indian
And more female
Less male
I was still
The outsider

By us was mother
With infant attached
A gooey blonde boy
Melted
On her hip
Mother said
Breast is always
Best
Just look at him
I did
But doubted

There was a supporting
Murmur
But one dissenter
Another woman said
Some of us can't do it
It was a fly
In the ointment

Thing to say
And stayed buzzing
In the atmosphere
The women will have to
Sort this one out
I thought

But it gave me courage
To say to myself
Maybe loud enough
For mother to hear
Well I was never
A breast milk man
Hadn't had the chance
It didn't kill me
And besides
That boy will have to
Toughen up
And mother
One day you'll have to find
A new line

We were still waiting
For the speakers
To get going
The breasts had slowed
Everything down
But the story
Had run its course

(Dream date: 27 October 2020)

Movers and Shakers

We were moving in
The whole family
But were we related
Mum Dad
Me
And the little brother

Things were stacked up
Inside
Waiting
To be unpacked
In fact
They'd already started
Spilling out
Everywhere
Connections were waiting
To be made

Our first sleep
Was a shocker
On the hard floor
Amidst the growing mess
I woke us early
After a hard night's day
Wrestling discomfort
Writhing even
Not dreaming the dream
I can tell you
A gastric reflux night
A stomach churner
Painful indigestion
Not getting on with it
The necessary sleep

I roused at 6.05 dreamtime
Said I'd have another go
At sleeping
Proves to be a promise
I couldn't keep

Everyone was now up
At the wrong time
Mother and father
Tried to be understanding
Or were silent about it
We were off
To a bad start
Oh well
Get on with it
The setting up
We rolled our sleeves
Up
At least I did

But things went
From bad to worse
It was all becoming
A hell of a mess
The walls were getting
Kicked in
Seems it was junior
Why wouldn't that kid
Respect this house
I nearly wanted
To throttle him

To really
Complicate things
Amidst all this
Growing disorder
And setbacks
There was an urgent task
To be done
Someone had to get the runt
A crimson business shirt
For the first day
Or perhaps night
At school

You'd have to take
The messy little blighter

With you
A job I wanted to avoid
At all costs
It didn't matter why
Take my crimson shirt
I said to mother
I could see my shirts
Unpacked hanging
Me the helper
But I was really
Helping myself
She saw through
My plan
The shirts remained
Suspended
I could feel her doubt
Hanging in the air
With them

Then to add to it
Comings and goings
And some kids
From who knows where

Growing exasperation
And oh that junior
Whose destructive plays
Were getting worse
He was building up for it
Yes I wanted
To gag someone
Maybe myself
If this went on
I could see where this was
Going

In the end
Father had to go out
For the shirt
It wasn't a great success
He returned

To the ruinous unpacking
In a real distemper
He was having it out
With mother
Giving her a piece
Of his mind
It was her fault
This disastrous move
How could you forget
The daylight savings difference
He bawled
We must have crossed
The Timezone
Stop talking over me
He bellowed over her

But I didn't hear mother
Say anything
In fact she was silent
Ensconced downstairs
In the kitchen

Meanwhile that kid
Was continuing to sabotage
Our settling
Wounding the house
With disarray and damage
I wanted to get him
By the neck

I felt a growing sense
Of suffocation
Incredulous and cross
We were losing the plot
The campaign
Everything I did
To put things in their place
Came undone
Will someone keep an eye
On
That brat

Imp
With a hard glint
In his eye
Must I keep my brother
On and on
It went

By this stage it all seemed
A terrible mistake
A painful conundrum
Was this house wrong
For us
Or were we
The wrongdoers
It was hard to say
It was time
To get out
Abandon ship
Sinking feeling
Drowning in the mess
The little perfidies
Of the youngster
And his confederates
The growing rancour
Of the parents

Could I fight my way
Out of this paper bag

Did I have the energy
After that terrible sleep
For this family plan
Going off the rails

Thankfully it ended
The project was cancelled
At about 2.30 am
I checked out
Said the clock

I'm lying in the dark
Gut sore
And undecided
Should I get up for antacid
It's in the kitchen
There could be
Consequences
I might get trapped awake
Unable to go back
To the dreamworld
This could be
A wrong footing

I mustn't risk a bad start
Was that the lesson
Of the dream

I slept a while again
And woke
Still in the dark
Still with that dream
In mind
I thought no
Its message is about
Time
But what about it
Perhaps we just have to go
With
It

Sleep again
Wake again
4.41
These micro snoozes
After the big dream
Are like searches
For what just happened
For the riddle of it
A whodunnit
I think

I must get back in time
Good luck with that
I wish myself

(Dreamdate: 29 October 2020)

The Buzz

The tradies are leaving
But tarrying
After working
On my flat
Will you please
Move on
I'm trying to have some
Quiet time
Off parade

But then
The lead man
Calls me out
Catches me
With my pants down
We move on
Even me
Don't cut me off

The fore man
Has an important message
I must pass on
To the planning consultant
An expert organising
The return of my place
To the order of things
Back to a good position

The man who speaks
The memo
Might be called Colin
But I dropped his name
Is he organising all this
Someone has to
I'm just fiddling about

There was a need
To relay a big dispatch
An order of some sort

Could I do it
The one in the middle
It was an urgent thing
Someone had to contact
Someone
About something
Two names too many
I was struggling
To catch it
And hold it
Hot coal
Potato
Mash up

But the message was out
In the air
The drums were roaring
A
Big
Note
Was coming through
The place was abuzz
With an arrival
Swarms of busy bees
Were hard at work
Announcing it
Orchestral
Portentous

I woke halfly in the night
The roar was the helicopter
At the Royal
Children's
Hospital
Nearby
Sick kids in the air
Arriving and going
Fixing the poor things
Putting them
In the right place
Yes that's a big message

I thought
We need to help
The wounded littlies

(Dream date: 3 November 2020)

The Road

I'm on a scrubby slope
Making my way down
To a clear flat
With someone
Who is it
She didn't say
Thinks there's animals
About
Back up the slope
I scan and watch
There's a bandicoot
On the ridge

Lost lover's children are
Nearby
Playing down
Another slope
I want to make them
Happy
Play a role
I call them up
Come see the natives
They respond to my call
The last up the ladder
The little one
Held
Guided
By big sister
As mother instructed

Mother
I'm outside her place
Looking inside
She's talking
To hubby
I'm waiting
Why

I'm packing my case
I'm a driver soon
I wonder how
She travels
Not like me
With silly suitcase
Something soft and round

I wait for her
What's she wearing today
A flash of her
But no appearance yet
Something white
With a collar

She comes
It's time to go
Where

The sadness
Is building
I see a bunk
In the first room
It's my bed
I want to lie in it
Let her watch me cry
Cry baby
For baby
Our baby
Lost

She's having none of
That
Asks breezily
Can you give me a lift in
Where

I want to
I don't want to
Go down this road
To nowhere
Again

(Dream date: 4 November 2020)

Falling Man

I'm at a large family
Gathering
In a big barn mansion
Must be one hundred people
But why exactly

A concert is getting up
In the huge shed
Pat's family seem involved
Looks like their musical tastes
Will be
On offer
Well that's intriguing

The audience
Arrayed
Waiting
Some rude people
Shoo me away
So they can see the show
The usual entitled smug set
Golf club types
I sneer
But it goes inwards
Up my arse

All this
I need a beer
An old lady serving
Tries to help
Risking the ire
Of the rude ones
I'm impressed
And moved
But it comes to nothing
We rummage
In the ice bucket
Only soft drinks
Bah

Lost lover is here
Somewhere
Dark and mischievous
Weaving in and out
The usual
I want to see her
But I'm anxious about it
Maybe I will get hurt
Again
It's always there
Lurking

I need that beer
I have a large
Guest room
Upstairs
With a well stocked fridge
I'll get one from there
In time for the show
And one for someone else
Who
I can't recall

En route
Who should I run into
But the ex wife
A startled moment
Together
I'm the most surprised
Why is she here
What's the connection
Just the old days
It seems
She's on a world tour
A victory tour
Seems across it all
Crossing it off
Still cross
With me

I head upstairs
Through lots of
Tooing and froing
Lost lover's eldest daughter
Is there
Mother can't be far away
Up to something
On a fun mission
With god knew who
It's all a lark

The lost wife is there
Has she tagged along
Or are we just tagged
And here is lost lover
She makes conversation
With the ex
Makes
An effort
Sing song
Fun song
I can only watch
It seems
A hard trinity
The ex and the lost
And me

Where's this going
Maybe
Over the top
It's building
But what's next
Are we edging
Forward
To the edge

I'm falling
Out of there
Awake
I feel like
I escaped
Something

(Dream date: 6 November 2020)

New Lover

I ran away
From the kids'
Sports carnival
With the married GP
We just decided to go
Left the nippers to it
And the ex
Bugger her

Someone tagged along
He wasn't always there
But then he was
Spoiling sport

It was and wasn't
A-okay
Excitement for sure
We tried to have a drink
Then a public announcement
Brendan Gleeson
Was missing
From the sports carnival
We laughed nervously

I can't find my phone
For the messages
Where the hell are you

She wants
A proper drink
We go to a pub
Full of scuffy patrons
Not a bad bunch
Can't find a table
We sit lie
Squeeze in
Does a beer come
Or not

Then it's time to sleep
Too late to get back
To the carnival
Point of no return
Give in

A messy night
The whole beer garden
Full of sleepers
In the morning she's cold
Even though it's not
Or maybe just needs
Extra covering

I get a blanket
From a helpful chap
Lying nearby
He sheds it
Like an extra skin
Good man
Doesn't cover her
Of course
She seems to be trying
To put it on
Like a glove
The woman next along
Keeps rolling onto the GP
She clearly has
Boundary issues

Constant anxiety
About that lost phone
And the messages
They'd be banking up
I've lost the bag it's in
The bag turns up
There's three phones
Including my first one
From years ago
None of them
Produce the goods

I'm still out of contact
With home base
Must be in the bad books
Like a library by now
Getting worse
I'm in for a real
Tongue lashing

It's time to go
That annoying man is back
Spoiler alert
He thinks he's in on this
Three's a crowd mate
Another one with
Issues
About who is who
And
What is where

The trinity parts
Heading back to our families
And heaven knows what
Must do this again
We three say
But then she breathes
Quietly to me
I want to see you alone
I feel a thrill

I start the long journey
Home
Hauling my trolley
Heavy loaded
But light hearted

What would I say
To the ex
And everyone
At home

Then
I know
What I have to say
It's my life
And I'll do things
Like this
I'm separated
From you
And myself

Sorry for the inconvenience
But I'm not apologising
Anymore

(Dream date: 11 November 2020)

Decisions

My daughter
About two years old
Was getting married
Ready to walk
Down the aisle
It would be happening
Soon

There she is
Through a glass window
We can see her
Radiant
I try to give her a kiss
Through the pane
But she really is on
The other side
What a pain

I must answer
The call of nature
Before the nuptials
Hurry
The procession
Is coming

The first toilet is flooded
And overflowing
Malign neglect
The second one is soiled
Awful
There's no way
Of cleaning it up
In time
Use it or lose it
The wedding that is
Sickening choice
Can't decide

Fades…

Next
I'm on the roof
Of the Royal Children's
Hospital
Helicopters are coming
And going
It's like a war film
Keep your head down
I'm looking around closely
One thing I notice
Is the absence of
Mosquitoes
They don't like
The choppers

You could live here
Mozzie free
Or take the buzzing
Back at my place
It's a choice

But it seems you can't avoid
A disturbed air
Anywhere

(Dream date: 13 November 2020)

The Black Sheep

I was outside
A large modern hall
An entertainment centre
Coming
Along the side of it
It was heaving
With a crowd
Of fundamentalists
I heard the speaker
Say my name
Refer to my new book
With Sam Alexander
Read it if you dare
The crowd roared
With laughter
Bugger you I thought

I needed to get inside
My disabled sister daughter
Was in there
A VIP guest
Of the gathering
In a special gallery
For special people
They treated specially
She was why they mentioned
My book

Father
Author
Black sheep
Of the family
Or maybe just
A honky
Astray

I was trying to get in
Of course
My pants were down

I was struggling to get them
Up
When a gaggle
Of teen aged schoolies
Turned up
A Sunday excursion
And went right in past me
It's a security thing
I pleaded with them
Struggling with my belt
They looked doubtful
I felt doubtful too

I got into the foreign event
And realised I was indeed
A standout
A strange writer indeed
I'd had my hair
Savagely pruned
A haircut
So I wouldn't need
A haircut
A practical bloke
Thing to do
Shorn like a sheep
Baa

Bah to all of this
Singing praising judging
I'll write my own stuff
Thank you

(Dream date: 17 November 2020)

His Natural Life

I was in the slammer
Banged up
For ten years
For some crime
I can't remember
It was early days
It was Santa Barbara
California
Back in the USA
Back in the USSR
Baby
With an ocean view

My cell's a mess
Even the bathtub is full
Of junk
Must do something about that
I've got lots of time
Years
Ten

Various adventures
Including a brief frolic
In the neighbourhood outside
We were teens again
Girls were along
For the rides
Doings in front gardens
Stirring up the citizens

The sarge and his gang
Come after us
He's disappointed
We are taken back
By the ears

That NCO is tough
But good hearted
We let him down

He takes us back
To the games room
He drops a fun machine
Aw c'mon sarge
Get our shit
Together

We come to a place
Where you can make things
Even have a barbeque
Greenberg is there
He has a family
On the outside
He's trying to produce
A frothing concoction
For us all
He'd done it before

It doesn't work
It's a flop
I wouldn't put him
In charge
Of anything
No green shoots

I think I'll make myself
A cup of tea
In the kitchen
You can do that
Self servery approach
This place isn't so bad
After all
And I might get out early
Get off lightly
While it's all still new
This story

I head along a passage
Some tricksy boys
Little devils
Are following me

They want mischief
I yell back at them
They turn into plasticine
Monster dolls
I wrangle them
Screwing the main fellow's head
Out of shape
It's no good
He's laughing out
The world is bad plastic
Good luck
And fuck you

I'm free of them
In the yard
But oh dear
It finally dawns on me
Hits me like a tsunami
Grabs me by the throat
I'm in prison
My sentence is long
No early release for you
Bub

What will everyone back home
Think
Especially her
Oh lost lover
The field is free of me
She'll go for it
If she hasn't already

I'm really lost now
Dead to the world
I'd loved
Did I

Shame
Hurt
Humiliation
It all comes back

The lost boy
So far away

Rising gagging panic
The walls are closing in
This is unbearable
I can't make it
This cannot be
What if this is really true

With a mighty effort
I shake myself
Out of the dream
A gaol break

Phew
A close shave
Yet again
Relief
To be out of there

But am I free
Hard to say
Need another word for it

(Dream Date: 20 November 2020)

The Lark

Lost lover was back
Last night
Wending her way
Through the dream
She was near me
Alongside
But not

We were hanging out
With someone else
A dreaming team
A trying trio

She was staying
With one of her sisters
The uptight one
With the uptight husband
Or was that
All of them

The hosts weren't happy
With the guest
Especially her sis
They didn't like her
Frolics

Lost lover reports this
To me
Rolls her eyes
What about that husband
She scorns
He even makes the bed

We were taking her
Back
To the hosts
In the car
My old bomb
At the petrol station

She solves the problem
Of the bill
With a special gadget
From the company
Insider trading
Flick
Of the switch

She buys some supplies
For the sister's family
In the garage shop
To appease them
The careless guest
Delivers
A few groceries
A loaf and nibbles
Breadcrumbs to scatter
She laughs
Rolls those sparkling eyes
Again

The family had been up
Since 3am
Tough on the guest
Maybe revenge
I thought

My heart melted
For her
Oh
You must be
So tired
I embraced her
Held her to me
It was like hugging
A postbox
Or maybe just
A traveller
Who doesn't have time
For this
Let go of me

I'm moving on
On the fly

From then
My heart was open
Unshielded
Its contents
Pouring out

As the dream went on
That old feeling
Was there
Where I was just
Letting it go
The love
Flooding away
To nowhere
And in came
The tide
Of sadness
Exchange of flows
As it goes
Along
The story
My gory story
No morning glory

Please stop it now
Someone
Hey Director
For godssake
Cut

At one point
Someone praised her
I said gosh
You should get that down
On letterhead

Even then
I still loved her

Wanted to help
The rich girl
The lost girl
Loss girl
Last girl
First girl
Womans girl

But it didn't matter
She laughed
It was all a lark
Always had been

She flew away

(Dream date: 24 November 2020)

Windows

One of those
Scrabble dreams
Busy meanderings
With people
Adults and children
Comings and goings
Ados about nothings
I was alone
In the crowd
Loner
With his car
And camp stuff

Riddles and puzzles
Inside the dream
At one point a GP tells me
Over the phone
That I'd need to take
Malaria medication
For a tooth condition
Six months
Could be a breakthrough
But to what

Lost lover was there
Also the kids
In her busy
You can wait
Way

So I waited
Politely
Charmingly
Even read
A funny story
To the little one

But it was too much
The show could not go on

Near the end
I was practising my speech
To say
I could never see her
Again
Finito
Finis
Sayonara

I was building up for it
But couldn't
Get a hold of her
Out of range
Shadowy
There but not

I woke
First thought was
Good luck
With that plan
My dreams
Are broken windows
She can come
And go
As she pleases
Forever

And she will
She's like that
She'd like that

(Dream date: 28 November 2020)

Lost and Found

A lover came back
A forgiving girl
I'd let go
Some years back
Now suddenly hello
Dream lovers
Again

We had doings
And then
We were doing it
A type of it
I was down on the job
And work it was
As it always is
Let's get you there
Baby
I kept my eye
On her prize

She laughed
With soft resignation
When I started it
I thought
This is more for you
Than me
That's her
Yielding again

Soft lover was invisible
Which was lucky
Because a mate
Turned up
And he was chatting
I couldn't speak
Muffled of course

She was silent
What was going on

At her end
Were we getting
Anywhere
After a while
She put a stop to it
Showstopper
A pity I felt
I wanted to please her
And let's be honest
So please me

Anyway this was news
A story of
Lost and found
A play back
Read all about it
Herald

Then inside the dream
I told my therapist
I had a new dream poem
To send her
Oh alright
She sighed
Go ahead
Charge me again

That surprised me
It shook me awake

(Dream date: 3 December 2020)

Crashing and Crushing

I was at the bottom
Of a very steep hill
My little son
Had just survived
A terrible crash
In his billy cart
A miniature 1930s racing car
Showy driver
A quarter flash
And three parts
Foolish

He careered down
Recklessly
Chasing another kid
In a flashy waggon
They were heading
To school
I watched in horror
But also anger
As he lost control
Heading for the busy road
Below
And surely
A deadly collision

At the last minute
He diverted
And hurtled into
A light pole
He bailed out
Just before it happened
Rolled and got up
Phew
I ran down
That steep slope
Admonishing him
But also said
Good decision sir

Not such a silly cart
After all

Then the hill becomes
A tallish building
It's time to catch the lift
Back up
There are two sides
Of the building
To go up in
The Australian side
The American side
The lift will travel up both
And get you
To the top floor
Where you need to go
To return to
But first you must choose
A side

I choose the American side
Everything is 1930s kitsch
On the ground it's a shop
Selling baseball memorabilia
Flashy
The Americans baby

The floor proceeds upwards
There's portentous organ music
The meister
Is at the controls
Somewhere above
On the Aussie side

Up and up
We go
Going
To the top floor
The best and last
One

Oh no
The American ceiling
Is lower
Than the other side
The rising floor
Will collide into it
I will be squashed
It's happening
It's really happening
I'm about to hit the roof
Squashed like a bug
Bugger

I scream out to the operator
Who is now my ex wife
Stop

Choking horror
There's no escaping this

Dream ends

(Dream date: 5 December 2020)

Sidelined

I waited for her
And waited for her
I waited
I waited
I waited

Diversions
Doings

I saw the empty bed
We slept in
And pondered
Her place
On the left side
But she always slept
On the right
For some reason
I could only see
The my side
Which was now
Hers
But she was gone
Doggone

My sister appeared
With many of my relations
She knew
I was in a mood
A distemper
Not paying attention
To the family
In this period of time
She seemed to know
That I was waiting
For resolution
Or maybe just bail
It lessened my crime
For now
She'd wait it out too

But then

At one point
I was at a kitchen sink
Some fool
Has removed the tops
From the taps
And large threatening
Bull ants
Were boiling
Out of the left one
I recapped the geysers
Or meant to
Wanted to
Did I

I waited for her
And waited for her
I waited
I waited
I waited

And
I woke
Heavy
With her
Who wasn't there
On her side of the bed
The right side
The left
Without a goodbye
Side

I slept briefly again
It was a swift
Deep divey sleep

I was wearing
A protective suit
And breathing apparatus
Someone was with me

Beside me
Similarly protected

I think I realised
During the last dream
That she's not coming

(Dream date: 8 December 2020)

Interruption!
His Mastering Voice Calls Out from the Balconies

We are near awakening
when we dream that we dream.
'Novalis', Fragments, per Thomas Carlyle

Womans Business

The Victorian government
Heroes of the pandemic
With a good
Social conscience
Announce that women
Won't be counted
In social distancing rules
In pubs and venues

The declaration shimmers
Like common sense
But is it

I hear
Different opinions
Deep in my head
It's pro women
Some voices say
It's pro venues
Others say

It's pro blokes
I think

An all female band
Take to the stage
The manager joins in
Singing
Squawking
I think
What a ruckus

Why not
Some voices say
She's helping
The sisters
Out
And she can now
It's the new rules

I'm staying out of this
They'll have to
Sort this out
Themselves
I'm only ever
An observer
Or maybe
Just a listener
Not even
In the audience
The stalls
I float in the ether

But that awful singer
No one could say
That's helpful
But I'm no one
And won't say anything

I'm on the sidelines
When it comes
To this question
Always

(Dream date: 9 December 2020)

Half Baked

The therapist
Turned into
An old lover
But which one

She was teaching me
How to
Make a pie
This went on for ages
She was very patient
And at the right moment
I took over
Smoothed it out
It was looking delicious
The family meal
This evening

Of course
At the end
Of the work
It turned
Back into sand
And soil
A gravelly
Grainy
Dish

All the while
I was anxious
For something
Happening
Or will happen
Outside the dream

A message
And probably
A bad one
From lost lover
Was brewing

In the post
I felt anxious
About what was ahead
After sleep
Would I wake to
Sadness
Knowing my luck

I asked the
Cooking instructor
For a cuddle
A bit of a snuggle roll
Gladly she obliged
And we embraced
Or wanted to
Did we

It all seemed
Half baked
The pudding
The embrace
Nothing was what it said
It would be

Later I'm at a party
The outsider
A photographer arrives
A surprise group portrait
Had been arranged
For the birthday girl
No one warned me
Caught with my
Track suit pants on
I was in the front row
Of course

I tried to control
The picture
Move the frame above
My waist
Luckily

At the last minute
Mother intervened
And stood in front of me
Cancelling me out

Father joked
Good naturedly
What about these danglers
From far away
I'm sure he included me
In that

I shot back
Well what about
The janglers
Because
That's what I really was
Attracting attention
That I didn't want

I was half dressed
With a showy wangler

(Dream date: 13 December 2020)

The Mendicant

I woke exhausted
From journeys
In foreign worlds
Estranged
In strange lands

It all started
Innocently enough
Or was it
I was entertaining
A friend's young daughter
Rides on my shoulders
When I decided
Like the show off I was
Or wanted to be
To start flying a little
Then it happened
We went over the cliff
And down the canyon
In a sickening swoop
Plunging through
And along
River valleys
That took us from
Our world

We arrived in a city
Possibly knowable
Probably Sydney
If things had gone
Another way
It was a place of
Ordered disorder
Facaded streets
With lurkers behind
Ruled over by
The authorities

They'd better not
Catch us
Runaways
Flight by nighters
Are not welcome
We must go undercover
Go to ground
A cover up

I'd left my mobile phone
In the homeworld
No contacting the base now
The who

I tried to use the eftpos
In the main drag
No deal
Sucker

The silent dream voice
Told me
An ex was living here
Had been for some time
Under an arrangement
I tried to contact her for help
But she banished me
Again
Women
Bloody kiwis

I came upon an exile family
Living furtively
And filthily
And they merrily took us in
Or were they just a bit
Idiotic
It solved the issue of
The lass
She joined in
With the wild kids
She was safe now
Wasn't she

The family didn't clean
Their filth
I had to
Of course
Felt compelled to
Scraping ordure
Off the plates
Got nowhere much
Trying hardly

Onwards
More journeys
In tightening circles
And increasingly indoors
The outsider on the inside
In busy homey rooms
But I was no closer to
Beddy beddy
And an end to this

The journey
Of renunion
Return to hearth
My world
Was feeling like
A losing cause
A loser's course

At one point
ABC radio Melbourne
Got in touch
For an interview
About my feelings
I did well
And it gave me
A temporary lift
But what did I say

The walls were closing in
I was lost in smaller places
With a few surprising breakouts

The radio quiz
Was on the driveway
Things ramped up
For a moment

And Pat
Turned up
In the backyard
Repeatedly galloping
A little horse
Or was it a mini mule
Up the paddock
And each time
Spearing it into the ground
Landing right on his head
The nearly bald noggin
Ouch matey
I had to say

He put his finger
To his lips
In a silent
Shoosh
Man's gotta have
His pride
And a few cracks
At it
The man's
A cracker

I was getting no closer
To home
Lots of pointless little
Side trips
No finish line
And as usual
There were no clean toilets
To hand

The rooms got busier
Which made the banishment

More intense
On and on it went
One thing leading
To another
And another
But never
Home

Then director called a halt
I woke at home again
Heavy with those lost worlds
And the child
I'd left behind

(Dream date: 16 December 2020)

The Formula

I was in a house
Full of things
Stuff stuffed
A few people about
Kids
Playing it out
In their corners

There was also
Visiting stepfather
Youngish
Modish
Super cool
Almost cold
But not quite
I was conscious
Of him
In my mind's eye

We were coming up
For 4 o'clock
When I would be going
Downstairs
For knee surgery
I wasn't anxious about
That work
It was the type
Where you're awake
And can chat to
The quack
A woman
I was half
Looking forward
To it
Not quite a date
But a bit of a
Prospect
You know what
I mean

I was delaying us
Our crew
Would have to leave
This house
One day soon
Give it back to
The owners
Who can't be too far off
We'd messed it up
Wronged the place
A little

Our kids
Were little grubs
But nice ones
Not mine
But close enough
To want to cuddle

I tried to pick up
The rubbish
Which was everywhere
You looked
You didn't want to do
That
Much
Because this seemed
To make it grow
Just peeking is best
Forget about the rest

Bit of foot tapping
In the background
I was going to make us
Late
But thought
It will be alright
Let's rely on
The rubber clock
And besides
Everyone was

Pretty relaxed
When you took
A closer look

I'd dressed up
For the doctor
Herself
But infuriatingly
The track suit bottoms
Had sneaked back on
Oh well
Start again
When on the stage
You want to pull
Your best pants
Down
No drama
In that

The bendy clock was
Wavering past the hour
Well let it
I must factor in
The loo
Before we go
Gentle sighs all round
Well you can't be
Caught short
During the procedure
Come a cropper
Be a flopper

The hip dad
A sigher
Had done his own
Necessary
This was a revelation
I'd stumbled into
On my rubbishy searches
There was quite a waft
No different to us

Stinker
After all

I was checking
The blemishes
We'd all made
Around the house
The messy guests
Especially the wall marks
That junior
Was working on
Little devil
Cheeky chap
Cutey really
Come here
For a squeeze
Nah play on
Do your best

I found house mother's
Wash cloth
Under the sink
Amidst the cleaning clutter
It was a dirty man's shirt
I set to work
On a few marks
Samples before
The big scrub ahead
They cleaned up nicely
Ah I thought
We will do this
Get the house
Back in order
For the owners
The away stayers

Right
We should be going
Down
For the knees up
Shouldn't we

But a clever idea
A formula
Comes to me
Out of all this
Garbagey housing

I seek out pongy dad
To lay the news on him
Hey bub
You know what the secret
Of managing houses like this
Is
I wink
You know
The houses of stuffers
We know who they are
He knew
No need to name
Names

Well I said
Pleased with myself
It's quantum in
And quantum out
Simple as that
Case closed
Publish that

He was a maths man
And therefore impressed
I'd hit the nail
On the noggin
On the right tack
Got the numbers right
The ducks were
Lining up

Now we could go
Down below
But would we

(Dream Date: 19 December)

The Wall

Oh no
I exclaimed to you
Masterful mistress voice
As I rushed back
I've left the lid off
The paint tin

I got back to
The site
My wall
And sure enough
Inside the tub
All was lumpy

The colouring project
Was only
Half finished
When we left on our
Errand
What was it
Mission
Unaccomplished

Earlier I'd been breezily
Applying the first coat
Cobalt blue
Chatting to you
As I laid it on
Someone
Had recommended
The colour
Was it you
Unusual
For an internal wall
Bluesy
Takes guts

I set back to work
With the clumpy brush

But it wasn't looking good
Streaky freaky
A botched job
Oh well
The light
Isn't very good
In this part
Of the house
In the bowelsy part
Might just have to
Live with it
Like everything else
In my place
I think I can settle
For this
Deep failing

I see little swipes
Of vibrant colour
Left by my departed
Mother in law
Whilst I was away
Working away
She'd snuck in
And dabbled
Tests
Alternatives
For the fix up job
Cleaning up after
The silly law son
Clearly
A whole new colour
Was needed

I pondered the verdict
Disagreed
No change of plans
I'm fine with this
The job was
Mine to finish

That other voice
Comes in
You say
I must paint
With the right emotion
Let it flow
From the heart
None of this busy chatty
Slap it on stuff
You've made
A blue
Blew it
It needs to blow over

I think
Thanks for the advice
But I'd rather
You pick up a brush

I step back
And behold
My handiwork
Perhaps it looks
Right enough
From a distance
Doesn't everything

I'm stepping backwards
To improve the view
Towards the exit
Can't get there
Quick enough

(Dream date: 21 December 2020)

Ship Shaping

Would I go on that cruise
To Europishy place
I wonder
I won't do aeroplanes
Anymore
Nasty
Suffocating things
Disturbing
The atmospheres
Especially mine

But a ship
That's travel I can do
And it's time for
An adventure
A slow safe one

My brother is
The captain
And shows me
Around the boat
He's a rough bastard
My room is a tough shed
And a long way from
The loo
It's quite a hike
He laughs
Unsympathetically

Now I'm not so sure
About this
Stuck with him
And inconvenience
On the long journey
It's not
Looking good

But then
My baby doll sister

Is coming along
Brother is much nicer
To her
She gets a better berth
I'm glad for her
She should be
Looked after
A cute little tot
Silently adorable

I'm really starting
To wonder
The journey now
Seems unappealing
A painy long haul
But if I don't go
I will miss little missie
The chance to
Get to know each other
Again
After our years
Of separation
This dilemma is tugging
At my heart

Back in the house
Father is angrily mopping
The kitchen floor
Mother is hovering
Maybe cowering
It's a rough scene
I feel censure
It's always there
In the home air
I grab a special cleaner
And try to tidy up
After pater
He rages onwards
I plough my own furrow

I'm tired of all this
Criticism and grimacing
It's time to leave
This difficult home
After all I have kids
Of my own
I need a change
Something must be done

If I move away
I'll always return
As the visitor
People would be nicer
But oh dear
I'd miss little sis
What to do

I carry out
The dirty kitchen door mat
For a good shaking
Sis appears
By my side
And takes up one end
But she's so small
And can't keep up
Her end of the bargain
The dirt spills away
To the wrong places

I'm not critical
She's my lovely girl
We've got a lot
Of catching up to do
And she needs
Big brother
In this unfriendly place
Wants an ally
Amidst this motley crew
A ship's mate

Next I'm in the family
Board room
For a reading of a will
Not a good will
Or maybe
It's just a real estate
Transaction
Filthy lucre
Who knows
Important family friends
Are there
Suited
Lawyered up

Sister is there
But now much older
Looking well
Must be excited
About the boat trip
She'll be ok
That is clear
The girl has made it
The inner circle
The cognoscente
She's found
Her niche
Left the losers
The losters

I join the high table
No jacket
And probably
Trackie pants
But at least
There was a good shirt
I just make the muster
A juster
I'm tolerated
But ignored

The room empties
Unsuits itself
Is it interval
Or are we
Further along
I stay behind
With soiled hands
Not good to go

Gruff friend appears
From his cave
In the north
I work on the paws
Nearly done
But some soil still
On the back of
One hand
Mr right
Is wrong
Gruffy growls
Aw come on
Clean yourself up
Man
Get ship-shape

Can I do this
Will I ever
Be unconstrained
Here
Ugh
Feels like
A familiar scene
An old question
Here
There
And everywhere

To my surprise
The caveman helps me
A little
Shoves

A soap dispenser
My way
It's nearly empty
But perhaps
There's just enough
For the job
I get to work
Sleeves rolled up
I think I can do this

Clear the decks
At last

It ends
I find myself still ashore
Awake

(Dream date: 21 December 2020)

Back Again

I was at a work centre
With my staff
An unfamiliar place
I was exhausted
Really collapsing
With it
The dead weight

At the meeting
To discuss the upcoming
Meeting
I lay down
Had to lean on the
Deputy director
I needed her help
Couldn't chair
The gathering
Needed a snooze
A long one
Drop off
Deep dive

Everyone starts for
The meeting room
Down in the bowels
Of the building
I'm staggering
Nearly finished
I pass a bedroom
Next thing I know
I'm in the bed
The door is closed
The gang must have
Left me
To sleep it off
The show went on
Without me
One director is flat
On his back

I'm asleep but
Awake
I know what's going on
But it's not a dream
Is it

Someone's dog
Has been left with me
It's on the bed
Going at my feet
Nipping them
Get off me
Annoying mutt
I want to shoo him
Away
But I'm immobilised
I cannot move at all
Not a finger or toe
Not even an eyelash
Dead to the world
But aware
I'm like the man
Who wakes
In his coffin
Nailed down

This goes on
For a long time
I try several times
To get myself moving
Mighty little efforts
Of will
Without power
They don't change
Anything
Nothing doing
A strange
And alarming
Time

Then finally
With one great

Uuurgh
I break the bonds
I rouse
I am free
I am awake

I remember
Junior
My little bloke
Oh dear
What happened to him
During my
Zombie slumber
Also
What went on
At the meeting
I must get up
To speed
Get cracking

I make my way
Into the central plaza
Must find my kid
And my people
I have work to do
Things to sort out
Balls
To pick up

Moving again
Back in the saddle
Where is everyone
What's the news
Bring me up
To speed

And hey kiddo
I'm coming for you

(Dream date: 25 December 2020)

Closing Scene
The Womans Sing the End

...I feel, observe! – I am human.
I fear my observations;
Oh, bloody quaking under stars! Oh, great scrutiny of the heart!
My step, my sound, my deepest sleep, my breath and
*   tone of pulse.*
My girl, my child. Oh, silence! Oh, great, inaudible
*   path of the earth!*
I am a human. I do not fear! I love destiny!

Magical Song, Walter Rheiner

Encore!
The Mans Agree

...I perceive all of this; the deep misery in which I lay, the bright happiness in which I fly in other hours;
    within me is the fear of the beaver; the hunger of the kangaroo jumping isolated under southern stars; my soul is an enclosure full of wild animals, full of lurking, angry monkeys and gnawing hyenas;
    and I am powerless, poor; I fall down before it like a naked savage who, in a hot daze and dark broiling swamps, hears the ball lightning rolling around Kilimanjaro; – and yet I cry and laugh and sing with cracked lips;
...and my heart glows like a pearl, and my eyes are diamonds: –
    My world! My great, dancing world!

Nocturne (Cologne), Walter Rheiner

Curtain Call
His Mastering Voice Wants
The Final Word

The first Man is the spirit-seer; all appears to him as Spirit.
What are children but first men?
The fresh gaze of the Child is richer in significance
than the forecasting of the most indubitable Seer.

Fragments, per Thomas Carlyle, 'Novalis'

The Mans Have it
Men Must Change

Men cannot remain children forever;
they must in the end go out into 'hostile life'...

The Future of an Illusion, Sigmund Freud

End

The Dreamer Wakes

We now have night vision
That much is clear
Imagine this deployed to life
As an ordinary thing

Womans, Mans
We need to pact
With a sleepless God
Or suffer His sighs

Think of dreaming
Where we wander unafraid
With the primals
Safe that we won't wake
To censure nakedness

For my part
I would finally abide
These nocturnes

Träume, Heinrich Vogeler, 1911

Found Much Later Scrawled on a Discarded Entry Ticket

By Baudelaire! Things are pretty hot!
Jacques Lacan

www.ingramcontent.com/pod-product-compliance
Lightning Source LLC
Chambersburg PA
CBHW040241010526
44107CB00065B/2827